The **MY-FUN-WITH-WORDS**

dictionary

by JAMES ERTEL

illustrated by GEOFFREY BRITTINGHAM
JOHN EVERDS

published by THE SOUTHWESTERN COMPANY

Nashville, Tennessee

DEDICATION

This dictionary is affectionately dedicated
to Jean, Chris, Scout and Herman.
They had the forbearance to put up with me during
the long months when it was being written.
(Forbearance is not in this dictionary, unfortunately.)
Scout and Herman got off lucky.
Scout is a collie, and Herman is a hamster.
They never had to help me over the rough places,
except by being pleasant and cheerful.
Jean is my wife, and Chris is our son. They often took time
from other things to read definitions I was not sure were clear.
They pointed out things that were wrong,
made suggestions, and gave cheering encouragement.
(Encourage is in this dictionary)

Design: Willis Proudfoot, Don Walkoe
Production: Robert H. Grigg

Dear Parents,

Children love to learn. They have vivid and incredible imaginations. They turn their imaginations loose on language in ways you and I can't fathom. They invent words, and they use old words to mean things you and I never thought those words meant.

That's great! Language is a living thing that belongs to the people who use it. Shakespeare and Lewis Carroll invented many words because they needed them. Standards exist, sure. And just as assuredly, a thing that is living grows and changes.

This dictionary was written with the sole idea of encouraging kids to feel free with words, to have fun with words, to enjoy words. The ability to use language is one of the most valuable skills your children can acquire.

Encourage that ability, and have fun along with them.

James Ertel

Dear Kids,

You know what an 🍎 is. Nobody has to tell you what an 🍎 is. You have eaten an 🍎, and you have probably seen many 🍎🍎🍎 on 🍎 trees.

You probably know most of the words in this dictionary. There may be some you don't know. For example, collide means this

Sometimes the words in this dictionary are used in strange and funny ways. That was done to show you different ways words can be used. Go ahead and invent your own.

Have fun!

James Ertel

abcdefghijklmnopqrstuvwxyz

aardvark The **aardvark,** believe it or not, is an animal that eats ants. Animals that insist on eating ants are called anteaters. Take an **aardvark** along on your next picnic.

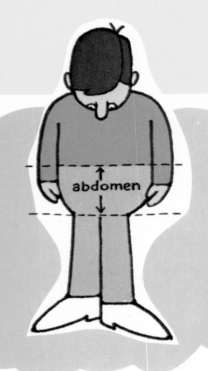

abdomen Your **abdomen** is that part of you between your chest and your legs. **Abdomen** is another word for belly. **Abdomen** takes longer to say than belly.

about **About** usually means almost. "I'm **about** as tall as that horse." Sometimes it means getting ready to. "The show is **about** to start." Sometimes it means other things. Don't worry **about** it.

abracadabra   This is a very special magic word which was used by the ancient Greeks. Nobody remembers what it was supposed to do. Try it a few times and see if anything happens.

accept   If somebody says, "Would you like this?" and you say, "Yes, thank you," you **accept** what he is giving you. It is always polite to say "Thank you" when you **accept** something.

ache   An **ache** is a pain in a tooth or a head or a stomach. Too much candy can give you a stomach **ache** or a tooth **ache.** Eat bananas.

achieve Achieve means to get something done. If you set out to build the biggest snowman in town, you **achieve** something.

across Across means from one side to the other. If you go from this side of the river to that side of the river, you go **across** the river. Always look out for cars before you go **across** the street.

active Somebody who is busy and moving is **active.** A cat running away from a dog is **active.** A father snoring on a couch is not **active.**

add If you have two fireflies and then catch two more, you **add** to your firefly collection. **Add** means to increase or to make bigger. In arithmetic the sign for **add** is +. It is called a plus sign.

address The number of the house or apartment you live in and the name of your street are your **address.** Always remember your **address** in case your parents get lost in the park.

admire If you think somebody is really great, you **admire** him or her. Think of the people you **admire.** There are also people who **admire** you.

9

admit If your father asks, "Who poured milk on the cat?" and your brother says, "I did," he **admits** doing it. To **admit** means to confess. To **admit** also means to let in. If you have a backyard circus and a neighbor kid comes with a ticket, you let him in. You **admit** him.

adult An **adult** is a fully grown creature. A puppy grows to be an **adult** dog. A butterfly is an **adult** caterpillar. Your parents are **adults.** You may understand **adults** better when you get to be one.

adventure If you capture a bunch of bank robbers, that is an **adventure.** An **adventure** is something that is exciting and dangerous. Sometimes crossing the street can be an **adventure.** Be careful.

advice When you ask somebody, "How should I train my pet gorilla?" you are asking for **advice**. You are asking him to tell you what he thinks you should do. If he tells you to get rid of your gorilla, maybe you should follow his **advice**.

affection If you like your parakeet, you have **affection** for him. You want to treat him well. **Affection** is a warm feeling you have for friends. **Affection** is a nice feeling that makes everybody happier.

afraid When it's dark and there are noises and you don't know what is going on, you may feel **afraid**. The scary sound coming from that tree is really just an owl. Mostly, people feel **afraid** when they don't know what is going to happen.

11

after You eat dessert **after** you finish your dinner. **After** means later or behind. If an alligator is **after** you, he is behind you. Keep it that way.

again **Again** means one more time. Climb a mountain. Go back down to the bottom. Then climb the mountain a second time. You have now climbed the mountain **again.**

agree "Let's have a picnic," your mother says. "That's a great idea," you say. You **agree.** To **agree** means to say yes to another person's idea or belief. If it is raining, it would be better if you do not **agree** to a picnic.

air Air is the stuff that goes in and out of you when you breathe. You can't see it or touch it, but it is all around you. **Air** that is going from here to there in a great hurry is called wind.

airplane A thing with wings up in the sky is either an **airplane** or a bird. If it has motors and makes a loud noise, it is an **airplane.** Birds do not have motors.

alive If a thing is **alive,** it moves around or grows. If your chair keeps getting bigger, it is **alive.** Usually, chairs don't do that. Chairs are not **alive.** Cats, trees, grass, and you are **alive.** Be glad you're **alive.**

alligator An **alligator** is a
long creature with four short legs,
a big mouth, and lots of teeth.
The next **alligator** you meet
may be friendly, but you can't
be sure about that. Never pet
a strange **alligator.**

alone When there is nobody
with you, you are **alone.** Sometimes
you want people to be with you, but
sometimes you want to be **alone.**

alphabet An **alphabet** is a bunch
of letters or shapes that are used
in writing a language. Our **alphabet**
starts with A and ends with Z.
Nobody knows why. We got our
alphabet from the ancient Phoenicians
who did it the same way. The ancient
Phoenicians never said why
they did it that way.

also Also sort of means this and that. "The donkey was big and **also** had a loud voice." Words are fun, and they **also** are interesting.

always Every day the sun comes up. The sun **always** comes up. It's good to know that we have a word called **always.** It's good to know the sun **always** comes up.

am I am. I **am** here. I **am** me. You are you. You are.

amazing If a cow ever really did jump over the moon, that would be **amazing.** Something that makes you say "WOW!" or "I can't believe it!" is **amazing.**

ambitious A kid hoping to eat a whole watermelon would be **ambitious.** A person with high hopes and great plans is **ambitious.** Tell everybody you're going to be President or Prime Minister some day.

among If you are with a bunch of kids, you are **among** them. To be **among** is to be part of a group. It's nice to be **among** friends.

amuse Tell a joke that makes your friend laugh. You **amuse** him. To **amuse** means to make happy or to entertain. Picking up a cat by the tail does not **amuse** the cat.

an This word means one. If you say, "I am going to eat **an** egg," that means only one egg, not two or three or twenty or one hundred forty eggs.

ancient Ancient means very old. The leftover pie in the refrigerator is not **ancient,** but a mountain is. Your aunt is not **ancient.**

and This word hooks two other words or ideas together. You might say, "I have an owl **and** a pussycat" or "I want a ham **and** cheese sandwich" or "You **and** I are friends."

angry When you get red in the face and want to fight or cry, you are **angry.** There are times when you should be **angry,** and times when you should not. To learn the difference takes some time and some patience.

animal Most people think an **animal** is a thing with four legs and fur. Actually, an **animal** is any living thing that is not a plant. That means grasshoppers, eagles, whales, and even you are all **animals.**

animal crackers Animal crackers are little cookies made in the shapes of elephants, lions, tigers, and other four-legged things. Dogs eat **"people crackers"** made in the shapes of mail carriers and police officers, dog catchers, and other people. The whole idea is rather silly.

ankle The place where your leg and your foot come together is your **ankle.** The bone that sticks out on your **ankle** is called an **ankle** bone. Doctors call it a talus. Doctors talk funny.

another Catch a rabbit. Then catch one more rabbit. You just caught **another** rabbit. Usually, **another** means one more, but it can also mean something different. If you have a blue horse and somebody gives you a green horse, that's a horse of **another** color.

19

answer "What is your name?" you ask. "My name is Abigail Arbutus Alicia Ampersand," she says. This is an **answer.** Not all questions are that easy to **answer.**

antlers The big horns on a male deer, moose, or elk are called **antlers.** They look handsome, but **antlers** are heavy. Nobody knows if a moose gets headaches from the **antlers.**

ants Ants are small insects that are always busy. It is not always clear what they are doing, but perhaps **ants** know. For such tiny things, **ants** are amazingly strong.

anybody "Is **anybody** home?" you call. **Anybody** means any person at all. If you get back an answer, "No," somebody is not telling the truth.

anything **Anything** might be in a strange box which you find. There might be a doorknob or a bird or a piece of pie or **anything**. Or, there might be nothing.

ape An **ape** is a very large monkey. **Apes** are quite smart and can be taught many things. In circuses **apes** ride bicycles.

apologize When somebody says, "I'm sorry I squirted grapefruit juice in your eye," he **apologizes.** To say you are sorry about something you did is to **apologize.**

appetite The feeling that you are hungry and want to eat is called **appetite.** Good smells coming from the kitchen can give you an **appetite.** Mud pies do not give you an **appetite.**

apple An **apple** is a round fruit that goes "crunch" when you bite it. Most ripe **apples** are red, but some are yellow. Green **apples** can make your stomach hurt.

are Are is the word that works with "you." You **are** healthy. You **are** happy. You **are** terrific. It can even work with "they." They **are** my sisters.

arm Your **arm** connects your hand to your shoulder. Your **arm** is a marvelous thing. It can bend and twist almost every which way.

around Around means on all sides and in every direction. The air is all **around** us. To walk **around** means to go in a circle.

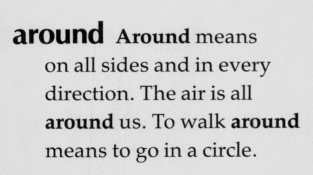

arrow "I shot an **arrow** into the air; it fell to earth I know not where" is from an old poem. Whoever shot that **arrow** was careless. Always be sure what you are doing when you shoot an **arrow.**

artist Many people think an **artist** is someone who paints pictures. Actually an **artist** is someone who does something very well. Someone who plants a beautiful garden is an **artist,** too.

ask "Where is my duck?" you **ask.** To **ask** is to say a question. To **ask** also means to request. "May I have another duck please?"

asleep When you are in bed at night and your eyes are closed, you are **asleep.** Sometimes when you are **asleep,** you dream.

astronaut Astronauts are people who travel in space ships. The word **astronaut** comes from old Greek words that mean star sailor. Would you like to be an **astronaut** when you grow up?

at At usually means that place. "I am **at** the castle." Sometimes **at** means in that direction. "I am looking **at** that pig."

25

atom Atoms are tiny, tiny things that are part of everything in the world. You have never seen one **atom,** but you have seen billions of **atoms.** You are made of **atoms.**

aunt A real **aunt** is a sister of your mother or father. **Aunts** are nice to have. They give presents on your birthday, and they seldom scold you.

autumn **Autumn** is the time of year that comes between summer and winter. Leaves change color and fall from the trees in **autumn.** Another name for **autumn** is fall.

abcdefghijklmnopqrstuvwxyz

baboon Baboons are large apes usually found in Africa. They have long noses and worried-looking faces. Nobody knows what **baboons** worry about.

baby A **baby** is a little thing that grows to be a boy or girl. Any very young animal can be called a **baby.** Your grandmother was once a **baby.**

back The part of you that you can't see is called your **back.** The first part of this book is the front, the last part is the **back.** When you come home after a trip, you come **back.**

bad Milk that has gone sour is **bad.** Things that are disagreeable or nasty are **bad.** Medicine may be unpleasant but it is not **bad.**

bake To **bake** means to cook in an oven. You can **bake** cakes, pies, and cookies in an oven. When you cook meat in an oven, that is called roasting. It's a strange thing, but that's the way it is.

ball In many games and sports you use a **ball.** A **ball** is roundish, but a foot**ball** is not completely round.

balloon The **balloons** that are used at parties and things like that are filled with air or some other gas. Before people had airplanes, they used giant **balloons** filled with hot air to ride up into the sky.

banana **Bananas** are good for you, but eat them anyway. If you ever saw **bananas** growing, you wouldn't believe it. They grow upside down.

bark A **bark** is the loud noise a dog makes. Some people say, "A **barking** dog never bites." Don't count on it. **Bark** also means the rough skin on the outside of tree trunks.

BARK!

baseball The word **baseball** means both the game and the ball that is used in playing the game. Many people get very excited about **baseball** games. Other people wonder what is going on.

bath A **bath** is something that many kids hate to get into, and then hate to get out of. A **bath** is a big tub of water that is used for cleaning all of you. People feel better after a **bath** because they feel clean.

beach A **beach** is the place where an ocean or a lake meets the land. **Beaches** can be either sandy or rocky. When you go to the **beach**, remember to take your **beach** ball and your sunscreen lotion.

beans Beans are tasty vegetables. They are actually rather large seeds. There are so many different kinds of **beans** that no one can name them all. They might be white, yellow, red, purple, black, or just about any other color you might imagine.

bear If you meet a **bear** in the woods, tip your hat and smile. **Bears** are large animals and they are very strong. People who know **bears** say you can't always be sure what a **bear** will do.

beaver Beavers build great dams in rivers and streams. **Beavers** and mice are cousins, but **beavers** are much bigger than mice. **Beavers** have big front teeth. The **beaver** is a symbol of Canada.

bed Bed is a place where you spend a lot of your time. Be glad you have a good **bed**. Pity the poor horse. Usually he sleeps standing up.

bee A wonderful insect is the **bee**. **Bees** make honey, and they help trees and plants to produce fruits and vegetables. **Bees** can sting. But if people let **bees** alone, **bees** let people alone.

before "I've driven a train **before**," you say to your friend. That means this is not the first time you have driven a train.

begin When the man says, "On your mark, get set, GO!" you **begin** to race. You start to race. When a seed sprouts, it **begins** to grow. When the sun comes up, a new day **begins.**

behave To **behave** means to do something in a certain way. You can **behave** nicely by closing the door quietly. Or, you can **behave** badly by slamming the door. When a grownup tells you "Please **behave,**" the grownup really means, "**Behave** the way I'd like you to."

bell Tiny **bells** tinkle, and big **bells** boom. Most **bells** are made of metal, but some **bells** are made of glass or clay. **Bells** are usually used for some kind of signal, like the one that tells you school is over.

belly button Your **belly button** is the dimple in your tummy. You can't button your shirt or your pants to your **belly button.**

belong "That ostrich **belongs** to me," you say. That means it is yours. You own it. "I **belong** to this club" means you are a member of the club. There are other ways to use **belong.** "Your hat **belongs** on your head."

below Farther down is **below.** The floor is **below** the ceiling. Your feet are **below** your head, unless you are a sloth. Sloths hang upside-down in trees. A sloth's feet are above its head.

belt The thing that goes around your middle and holds your pants or skirt up is a **belt.** A **belt** can be made of leather, cloth, beads, metal, or elastic. Always fasten your seat **belt** when you ride in a car.

Strawberries   Blueberries   Blackberries

berry A **berry** is a good-tasting fruit that goes great with cereal. A ripe **berry** is usually red, blue, purple, or black.

bicycle A **bicycle** has to have two wheels. The bi- part of the word means two. A thing with three wheels is a tricycle. A thing with only one wheel is a unicycle. Those are hard to ride. Be glad if you can ride a **bicycle.**

big A thing is **big** if it is large for its kind. A three-foot-high canary would be **big,** but a three-foot-high elephant would be small.

bird If you see a live thing with feathers, it has to be a **bird.** **Birds** have two feet and two wings. Most **birds** can fly, but some cannot. **Birds** come in many sizes.

birthday The day when you were born is called your **birthday.** Every year, when that day comes around, you celebrate your **birthday.** If today is that day, have a HAPPY **BIRTHDAY!**

bite Bring a hamburger up to your mouth. Crunch down with your teeth. That is a **bite.** It is not polite to **bite** your dentist or other helpful people.

black When you are in your bed at night and turn off all the lights, your room goes **black.** Some cats are **black.** Some people have **black** hair or **black** eyes.

blanket The thing that you pull over you in bed at night is a **blanket.** A **blanket** covers the whole top of your bed. In cold places, snow **blankets** the ground in winter. It covers the whole ground.

blood The red stuff that comes out when you get a cut is **blood**. **Blood** keeps your body going. When you lose some **blood** from a cut, your body makes more.

blow If the soup is too hot, **blow** on it. **Blow** a horn. **Blow** up a balloon. The wind **blows** the autumn leaves from the trees. To **blow** means to push air around.

blue **Blue** is the color of a clear sky. **Blue** is the color of a bright **blue** jay. Some balloons, flowers, and lakes are **blue**. Maybe your eyes are **blue**.

body The arms, legs, head, chest, and belly of you are your **body.** The **body** of a raccoon is the whole raccoon. **Body** usually means a whole animal.

bone Bones are those hard things inside your arms and legs and chest and head. If you didn't have **bones,** you could not stand up. A jellyfish has no **bones.**

book You are looking at a **book.** A **book** is made of paper, ink, glue, and other things. A **book** can entertain you, or a **book** can help you learn. A good **book** can do both things.

GHOST STORIES

boots **Boots** are what you wear in the winter when it snows. If you live in a place where it doesn't snow, maybe you never saw **boots**. **Boots** are things that cover your shoes and part of your legs.

both "I will see you **both** tomorrow," you say to Jill and Jack. **Both** is an easy word. It always means two.

bounce Throw a ball down to the ground and it comes back up. That's **bounce**. Some balls do not **bounce** very well. Cannon balls and meat balls hardly **bounce** at all.

bowl A deep dish that you eat cereal or soup from is a **bowl.** A place where football players play is often called a **bowl.** That's not as dumb as it sounds. A place where football players play has a shape like a **bowl.**

box A **box** is something to put something in. That's the only reason anybody would make a **box.** For a flea you need only a little **box.** For a whale you need a big **box.**

boy A **boy** is a creature that grows up to be a man. If you are a **boy,** be glad of it. If you are a girl, be glad you are a girl.

brain You will never see your **brain**. Your **brain** is inside your head, behind your eyes, and between your ears. Your **brain** runs your whole body. Everything you do, feel, and think comes from your **brain**.

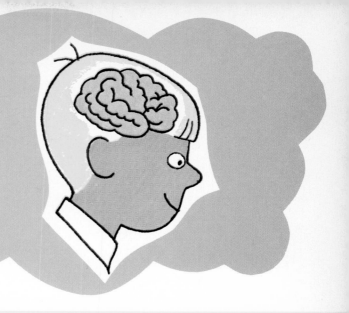

brave "I will save you from that snake," you say. That is being **brave**. To be **brave** is to try hard to do what you think is right, even though you know you might lose.

bread **Bread** is the stuff that is on the top and bottom of sandwiches. **Bread** is made of flour and other things. It smells great when it is baking. Learn to make **bread**.

break If you have a whole thing and suddenly make it into pieces, you **break** it. If you drop an egg on the sidewalk, it **breaks.** When you **break** something, it is usually an accident.

bridge A **bridge** is a good thing to get you from one side of a river to the other side without getting wet. There is also a card game called **bridge.**

bright You can't stare at the sun because it is too **bright.** A **bright** thing gives off a lot of light. If people think you are smart, they say you are **bright.**

bring "**Bring** your piano to my party." To **bring** means to take along with you.

broccoli **Broccoli** is one of those green vegetables that is good for you. Actually, **broccoli** tastes very good too! **Broccoli** is really a bunch of buds.

broken Something that is **broken** is in more pieces than it is supposed to be or it no longer works. Some **broken** things, like arms and toys, can be mended, but **broken** promises are hard to fix.

brother Be glad if you have a **brother,** even if he is bigger than you. A **brother** is a male with the same parents you have. If your mother or father has a **brother,** that **brother** is an uncle to you.

brown Brown is the color of chocolate, dead leaves, and a lot of horses. If you want to make the color **brown,** mix together yellow, red, and blue paint.

brownie A **brownie** is a thin chocolate cake that has nuts and other good things in it. A **Brownie** is a young Girl Scout.

brush You clean your teeth or untangle your hair with a **brush.** There are **brushes** all over your house. They are used for cleaning, painting, and fixing things up.

bubble A **bubble** is a roundish thing filled with air. You make **bubbles** in your bathtub, and you can blow **bubbles** with some kinds of gum. **Bubbles** usually don't last very long.

bug A small creature with a lot of legs but no bones is called a **bug. Bugs** like mosquitoes and flies can fly. **Bugs** like grasshoppers and fleas can jump. **Bugs** like ants have to walk everywhere they go.

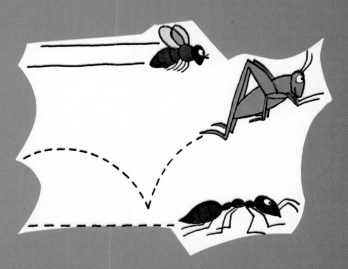

build To put a bunch of things together and make something is to **build.** Usually, you use wood, stones, or bricks when you **build.** You don't **build** a cake or a hamburger.

building A **building** is a thing that has been put together with many pieces according to a plan. Your tree house may look unusual, but it is a **building.**

bus A thing that is made to carry a large bunch of people along a street or highway is a **bus.** A **bus** has to have wheels, or it can't go anywhere.

busy When you have a lot of things to do and you are doing them, you are **busy**. **Busy** means you can't do anything else right now. You probably never get too **busy** to eat dinner.

butter **Butter** goes with bread, biscuits, pancakes, and corn-on-the-cob. **Butter** is made from milk, unless it is peanut **butter,** which is made from peanuts. Apple **butter** is made from guess what?

button A **button** is a round thing that is used to fasten pieces of your clothes together. A **button** that doesn't have a buttonhole to go with it is just a decoration.

buy When you give a storekeeper money for a penguin, you **buy** the penguin. When you **buy** something, you give money for something.

buzz Bees **buzz** and buzzers **buzz** and some kinds of machines **buzz**. A **buzz** is a low, soft sound that goes on and on.

by This is a small word that has a lot of meanings. Sometimes it means how. "I came **by** dog sled." Sometimes it means near to. "I went **by** that place yesterday." Sometimes it means other things. "I'll be there **by** two o'clock."

abcdefghijklmnopqrstuvwxyz

cabbage   A **cabbage** is a large, round green or red vegetable that looks a bit like a bowling ball. A **cabbage** is a bunch of leaves that grow tightly together. **Cabbage** is a tasty vegetable, but a bad bowling ball.

caboose   The last car on a freight train is called a **caboose**. There are beds and a stove in a **caboose**. The train crew lives there. If you live in a **caboose,** your view keeps changing.

cactus   A **cactus** can live in hot, dry, desert places where other plants can't. The **cactus** has a secret. It saves up water in its broad leaves. It has sharp spikes to keep animals from stealing its water.

cage When you put your goose into a **cage,** you put her into a thing she can't get out of. You can see her and she can see you, but she can't get out. Zoos use lots of **cages.**

cake A **cake** is a special dessert, so we sometimes have **cakes** for special occasions. Maybe it's somebody's birthday. Maybe it's because friends are there. Maybe it's a holiday.

calendar A **calendar** is a thing that lists all the days in a year. A **calendar** has your birthday on it, the day a friend comes to visit, and days when nothing much happens at all. Be glad for all the days on the **calendar.**

53

calf A baby cow is called a **calf.** A baby whale is called a **calf,** too, even though it doesn't look much like a baby cow. The back part of your lower leg is also called a **calf.**

call "Where is everybody?" you **call.** That meaning of **call** is to say something in a loud voice so everyone can hear. **Call** has other meanings. "I'll **call** you tomorrow," is one of them.

camel If a **camel** drinks your lemonade, that means he is very thirsty. **Camels** live in desert areas, and can manage to live for many days without water. There are **camels** with one hump, and **camels** with two humps.

camp You live in a home, but you stay in a **camp** for just a while. Soldiers stay in **camps,** and some kids stay at **camps** in the summer. There are things called **campers** that people live in during vacation.

can "I **can** catch that dinosaur," you say. **Can** means you are able to do it. "I **can** climb that tree."

canary Canaries are small birds that are yellowish. If your **canary** is purple, what you have is not a **canary.** Most **canaries** sing a lot. Be glad they are not great big birds, because they would keep you awake all night.

candle A **candle** is a fat string with a lot of wax around it. When somebody sets fire to the string, it burns and gives off light. **Candles** are cheery, and are used at celebrations.

candy Candy is that sweet stuff your dentist tells you not to eat too much of or it will ruin your teeth. Save your **candy** for a special occasion.

cane A stick people use to help them in walking is called a **cane.** The plant sugar is made from looks like a long stick, and is also called a **cane.**

canoe   A **canoe** is a long, skinny boat. Indians used to hollow out a log to make a **canoe.** Much of this country was explored by people traveling in **canoes.**

cap   A small hat that sits on top of your head is called a **cap.** The metal thing on top of a bottle of soft drink is also called a **cap.** When you take the **cap** off a bottle, it goes sssssssss. That doesn't happen when you take the **cap** off your head.

capture   If you catch a rabbit, you **capture** it. **Capture** is another word you can use if you get tired of saying catch.

car If you have to get twelve hippos from here to the next city, you can put them in a railroad **car.** A **car** is any thing with wheels that carries hippos, potatoes, or people from here to there.

careful Being **careful** means "Don't do that," and many other things. It means to stop and think a minute before you do something. If you are **careful,** you keep out of a lot of trouble. Be **careful** not to carry too many plates.

carnival A **carnival** is a fun time or a fun place. A time when there are parades and parties is a **carnival.** A place where there are games and rides and excitement is a **carnival.**

carnivore You eat hot dogs and hamburgers, and that makes you a **carnivore.** A **carnivore** is any creature that eats meat.

carpet That cloth stuff on the floor is called a **carpet. Carpets** are hard to clean. You can wipe your feet, but your dog may not remember.

carrot A **carrot** is a long, reddish root that grows below ground. You can eat **carrots** raw or cooked. Rabbits go crazy about them.

carry You may decide to **carry** your tuba to school. To **carry** means to take something from one place to another place. A truck **carries** pies from this place to that place.

cartoon A **cartoon** is a picture that is meant to be funny. If you draw a picture of yourself with a pigeon on your head, that would be a **cartoon,** unless you normally have a pigeon on your head.

cat A **cat** is one of those smallish, furry animals you see every day. Lions and tigers are relatives of the household **cat** and are also called **cats.** Only pet small **cats.**

catch "I've got it," you say, chasing after a high fly ball. When the ball comes down, if you grab it in your hands, you **catch** it. To **catch** means to capture or get hold of. If you can run very fast, you can **catch** a rabbit.

catfish A **catfish** is a kind of fish that has things that look like whiskers on its face. These "whiskers" make a **catfish** look a little like a cat, but not much. Any cat would love to eat a **catfish.**

cauliflower A **cauliflower** is a white vegetable. It is actually a bunch of tight flower buds. A **cauliflower** is in no way related to a collie. A collie is a dog.

cause If you do a rain dance, and make it rain, you **cause** it to rain. To make something happen is to **cause** it.

cave If you can't build a house, you can live in a **cave**. A **cave** is a large, long hole in the earth. A bear will live in a **cave,** if he can find one. A **cave** protects the bear from wind and snow.

celery Most people prefer to eat **celery** raw. **Celery** is the green stem of a plant. If you are trying to hide from someone, don't eat **celery**. **Celery** makes a lot of noise when you eat it.

CRUNCH!

cent Most coins are silver colored, but one of them is brownish. That one is made of copper, and is called a **cent.** Another name for **cent** is penny. You can buy a small piece of candy for a **cent,** but not much else.

center, centre* That place where the seeds are in an apple is the **center** of the apple. The **center** is the middle of something. There is nothing in the **center** of a doughnut.

certain "I am **certain** that ice is slippery," you say. When you say you are **certain,** that means you are absolutely sure. You are **certain** because you have seen a lot of people fall down on that ice.

chair A **chair** is a thing for one person to sit on. If it is long, and a lot of people can sit on it, it is a bench or a sofa. A **chair** that is fastened to the floor in a theater or an airplane is called a seat.

chalk **Chalk** is a powdery stick that is made mostly of ground up seashells. Most **chalk** is white, but it comes in colors, too. Use **chalk** to write on a blackboard or chalkboard, not on the living room wall.

champion If you win the peanut pushing race, you are the **champion.** To be a **champion** is to do better than anybody else, and to win first place. If your turtle wins first place in a turtle show, he is a **champion** turtle.

chance If you are captured by a giant and then he turns his back to you for a minute, you have a **chance** to run away. **Chance** can also mean maybe it will, maybe it won't. "There's a **chance** my frog can win the race."

change "Why don't we go to the South Pole this year for a **change?**" your father says. He is tired of going to the North Pole. To **change** means to make something different from the way it was.

chase A mouse that is trying to catch a cat is **chasing** the cat. It is a bad idea for a mouse to **chase** a cat. Advise your mouse not to **chase** cats.

chat People sitting around talking about this or that in a friendly way are having a **chat.** If they start yelling at each other, then they are having an argument, not a **chat.**

cheap "You can buy this genuine magic lamp for only five cents," says the storekeeper. That price is **cheap**. You thought you would have to pay more. **Cheap** can also mean not very good. "This **cheap** watch doesn't work."

cheer The happy yell you give when you have your favorite food for dinner is a **cheer.** A **cheer** is a glad shout that people give at a ball game when their team wins.

cheese A rat might tell you that **cheese** is his favorite food. **Cheese** is a tasty food that starts out as milk. There are a lot of different kinds and flavors of **cheese.**

cherry A **cherry** is a small, roundish fruit that grows on a tree. A **cherry** might be yellow, red, or purple. A **cherry** has a hard, round seed in its center. It is not true that if you swallow a **cherry** seed a **cherry** tree will grow in your stomach.

chest Your **chest** is that bony upper part of you from your shoulders down to your belly. Your heart and lungs are in your **chest**. A **chest** is also a kind of box where you keep things.

chew When you put food in your mouth and break it into little bits with your teeth, you **chew** it. If you **chew** your food well, your stomach can digest it easier. **Chewing** gum is sneaky. It does not break into little bits.

chicken A **chicken** is a delicious bird that farmers raise for food. From the **chicken** come eggs and drumsticks. A whole bunch of **chickens** is called a flock.

chief An Indian **chief** is the head man, or boss, of the tribe. If you are the president of your club, you are the **chief**. Being a **chief** doesn't mean you get to boss everybody else around. Very often a **chief** winds up doing most of the work.

child Anybody who is still growing is a **child**. The time when you grow is called **childhood**. **Childhood** is an exciting time of learning and discovering many things.

chilly An autumn wind blows. You forgot your jacket. You feel **chilly**, and you shiver. When the weather is **chilly**, it is cold but not freezing. Go home and get your jacket.

choose "Give me that goat, please." When you pick one thing out of two or more, you **choose**. To **choose** means you like that thing better than the others. Nobody ever **chooses** right all the time.

circle A bicycle wheel, a dime, and a ring on your finger are all **circles**. A **circle** is a line that is perfectly round.

circus "I am going to join the **circus** when I grow up," you say. A **circus** is a traveling show with clowns, animals, acrobats, and a band. A **circus** is exciting, but it is hard work for the people who are in it.

city If you live in a **city**, you will probably never get to meet all your neighbors. A **city** is a very large town with thousands of people living close together.

clay Clay is stiff, mushy stuff that you can push into any kind of shape and it will stay that way. You can make a statue of your pet frog with **clay,** if you can get it to stay still long enough.

clean After you have been trying to sail paper boats in your favorite mud puddle, you are definitely not **clean.** You will need to **clean** up. That means, wash all that dirt off you, and put on **clean** clothes.

clear On a sunny day when the air is **clear,** you can see for miles. Something that is **clear** is something you can see through. You can see through a glass of water because it is **clear.** You cannot see through a glass of milk.

climb Jack had to **climb** a beanstalk to meet the giant. When you **climb**, you go up. Don't **climb** up anything unless you are sure you know how to get down.

clock A **clock** measures time. Time moves, and that is why the hands on a **clock** move. An alarm **clock** tells you when to get up, and a school **clock** tells you when to go home. If your **clock** strikes thirteen, it is time to get your **clock** fixed.

close If you are so near an elephant that you can touch it, you are **close** to the elephant. If tomorrow is your birthday, your birthday is **close.** Get away from that elephant. He might accidentally step on you.

closet A **closet** is a place where you are supposed to hang your clothes or store your toys. A **closet** is just a small room that is meant for putting things in. Grown-ups sometimes hide presents in **closets.**

cloth Cloth is what your clothes are made of (except your shoes). **Cloth** bends every which way, and you can be glad it does. Iron pants would be heavy, and very uncomfortable.

cloud A puffy white thing up in the sky is called a **cloud.** Most **clouds** are made of tiny drops of water or ice. A few **clouds** are made of smoke or dust. A low **cloud** that touches the ground is called fog.

clown A **clown** is an actor who tries to make people laugh. **Clowns** wear strange clothes and painted faces, and do odd things. It is okay to laugh at a **clown.** When you laugh, the **clown** feels good.

cold When the temperature is so low that your snowman asks for a sweater and earmuffs, it is really **cold. Cold** means without heat. If your snowman says he is **cold,** he knows what he is talking about.

collar A **collar** is a thing that goes around a dog's neck. There is also a **collar** on your blouse or a shirt. You fasten a leash to your dog's **collar,** but your dog doesn't usually fasten a leash to your **collar.**

collect "I have more lemons than anybody else in the neighborhood," says your friend. He **collects** them. Every time he finds one, he takes it home. It is not a good idea to **collect** elephants unless you have a very large yard.

collide If you are running fast, and smack into a goat coming the other way, you and the goat **collide**. To **collide** means to crash into something with a great bump. **Colliding** can be bad for your health.

color Color is a word that tells something about the way a thing looks. The sky is blue, grass is green, and bears are black, brown, or white. People are of different **colors**, but they are all people.

colossal If your kitten should grow to be ten feet tall, it would be **colossal.** A **colossal** thing is a huge, giant thing. Your kitten probably looks up at you and thinks you are **colossal.**

comb A **comb** is a flat thing that you use to smooth your hair and make it look the way you want it to. The thin pointed things on your **comb** are called teeth, but your **comb** never goes to the dentist.

come "**Come** here quick!" you call to your friend. **Come** means you want him to go from the place where he is to the place where you are. You want him to **come** and see the big bug you found.

comedy A TV cartoon that makes you laugh is a **comedy**. Any kind of a play or show that means to be funny is a **comedy**. If you like to laugh, watch **comedies**.

comfortable If you are not hungry, and you don't itch or hurt, and you are warm enough, you are **comfortable**. You are **comfortable** when you are feeling good all over. Somebody reading you a story on a cold night makes you feel **comfortable**.

complete When you fit in the last piece of a jigsaw puzzle, the picture is **complete**. Everything is there. Nothing is missing. A thing is **complete** when it has all of its parts.

confess "I cannot tell a lie; I chopped down the cherry tree," said George Washington. If you admit you did something wrong, you **confess.** It is always better to **confess** than to say you didn't do something that you did do.

confident "I'm sure I can win this skating contest." If you know you are a good skater, and feel sure you can win, you are **confident.**

connect If you tie your wagon to your friend's wagon, you **connect** the two wagons. **Connect** means to fasten two or more things together. If you got all the wagons in your town and **connected** them all together, you would have a very long chain of wagons.

cook When you put a pan of food on the stove or in the oven or microwave, you **cook** the food. Remember to turn on the heat. To **cook** food you have to use heat. A hamburger won't **cook** on a cold grill.

cool It feels good to get **cool** on a hot summer day. A shady place and a tall glass of lemonade with ice cubes can make you feel **cool.** A heavy sweater won't.

corn **Corn** is a vegetable much loved by pigs, kids, crows, and other creatures. **Corn** grows on "ears," which sounds strange. **Corn** is actually a kind of very tall grass.

corner "I'll meet you at the **corner**," says your friend. A **corner** is a place where two streets cross, or where two walls come together. Don't get caught in a **corner** when you are playing tag.

cost "How much does that yo-yo **cost**?" you ask. You want to know how much money you have to have to buy it. "It **costs** fifty cents," says the storekeeper. "Wow," you say, "that's a lot of money for a yo-yo.

costume All those weird clothes you wear on Halloween are a **costume**. Actually, a **costume** is any style of clothes. The clothes you wear every day would look like a strange **costume** to somebody who lived in North America 200 years ago.

cotton A lot of the clothes you wear are made of **cotton**. **Cotton** cloth is soft and comfortable and strong. **Cotton** makes much better clothes than wrapping paper would.

cough That tickly feeling in your throat that you can't stop makes you **cough**. When you **cough**, you force a lot of air out of your lungs. Cover your mouth when you **cough** so you won't spread germs.

count ''There are five squirrels in my bathtub,'' you say. When you **count,** you find out how many. Usually you **count** by naming off numbers in regular order, until you have **counted** all the things you are **counting**.

country A **country** is the nation you live in. You may live in the United States or Mexico or Canada. **Country** also means a place where there are farms, woods, fields, ponds, cows, rabbits, frogs, and grasshoppers.

courage **Courage** is what you have when you say to a big bully, "I won't let you pick on my little brother." **Courage** is sticking up for what you think is the right thing to do even when it is hard to do.

cousin A **cousin** is a son or daughter of one of your aunts or uncles. An aunt or uncle is a sister or brother of your father or mother. It all sounds very complicated.

COW A **cow** is a large, heavy animal that eats green grass and turns it into white milk. Nobody knows for sure how a **cow** does this. **Cows** don't talk about it.

coward A person who seems to be afraid of everything is called a **coward**. Just because a person is afraid sometimes does not make him a **coward**. It makes good sense to be afraid of an angry bull.

cracker A **cracker** is called a **cracker** because it goes "crack" when you bite it. A **cracker** is a thin and crunchy thing that is made mostly of flour. If you eat **crackers** in bed, the crumbs will make you uncomfortable all night.

cranky "I don't like you anymore," says your friend. Your friend is **cranky**. Somebody who is **cranky** is unhappy and in a bad mood. Maybe your friend is tired or sick.

crash If you throw a ball, and it hits a window, you may hear a **crash**. A **crash** is a loud noise that usually means something just got broken. When cars hit, they **crash**. The sound of a **crash** usually means bad news for somebody.

crib A **crib** is a small bed with bars on it that a baby sleeps in. A **crib** is fine for babies, because it keeps them from falling on the floor.

crocodile A smiling **crocodile** has so many teeth that he can't close his mouth properly. A **crocodile** is a cousin of the alligator, but he is bigger and hungrier. It is a good idea to cross the street when you see a **crocodile.**

crow Don't try to feed your **crow** bananas, because **crows** prefer worms, bugs, and seeds. A **crow** is a large, black bird who is no good at all as a singer. It is hard to be a good singer when all you can say is "Caw."

crowd If all you can see are legs and feet, you are in a **crowd**. A **crowd** is a great bunch of people. A **crowd** is really a great bunch of anything. Five thousand reindeer would be a **crowd** of reindeer.

crown A **crown** is a heavy metal hat that a king and a queen wear. A **crown** is supposed to be a sign of power, but it is no good for keeping the rain off your head. Use an umbrella.

cry Babies **cry** when they are hungry, wet, or tired. **Crying** is the only way they can let their parents know something is wrong. Older kids and grownups **cry** when they are in pain or sorrow. Sometimes people **cry** at weddings because they are happy.

cub A baby fox, or lion, or bear is called a **cub**. A beginning Boy Scout is called a **Cub** Scout. None of these **cubs** looks like any of the other **cubs**. Nobody can figure out how they all got named by the same word.

cucumber "My **cucumber** will grow up to be a watermelon," Charlie says. That will never happen. **Cucumbers** and watermelons are plant cousins, but watermelons grow bigger and sweeter. A lot of **cucumbers** get made into pickles.

cup Your **cup** has a handle on it, and that makes it different from a drinking glass. If your **cup** doesn't have a handle, it got broken off somehow.

cupcake Your **cupcake** doesn't have a handle on it, but it was baked in a small pan shaped something like a cup. You can't eat a whole cake, but you can eat a **cupcake**.

curious "I wonder what is on the other side of that hill," you say. You are **curious**. You want to know. Maybe there is somebody else on the other side wondering what is on your side of the hill. He is **curious**, too.

cute If someone tells you, "I think you're **cute**," just smile. It means the person likes the way you look. Kittens and puppies are **cute**.

cylinder A soft drink can is a **cylinder**. A **cylinder** is a shape that is round and long. A lot of drinking glasses are **cylinders**, and so are round oatmeal boxes. There are lots of **cylinders** in your house.

abcde**d**efghijklmnopqrstuvwxyz

daily If you walk your pig to the park every day, you do it **daily.** A newspaper that comes out every day is a **daily** paper. Something you do every day you do **daily.**

dairy Don't expect to find kangaroos at a **dairy.** A **dairy** farm is a farm where cows are raised for milk. A **dairy** store is a place where milk, cream, butter, cheese, and ice cream are sold.

damp "My clothes are **damp,**" you say. They didn't dry completely after they were washed. They still have some water in them. Hang your **damp** clothes up to dry.

dark You can't even see your hands in the **dark.** When it is **dark,** there is no light and you can't see anything. **Dark** also means colors, like black, **dark** brown, **dark** blue, and **dark** green.

day **Day** has two meanings. One meaning of **day** is the time when the sun shines and you can be outdoors. Another meaning of **day** is a whole 24-hour period, from one midnight to the next midnight. It seems strange that a new **day** begins in the middle of the night.

decide "I don't know if I would rather have those skates, that monkey, or that pumpkin pie," you say. It is hard to **decide.** To **decide** is to make up your mind about something. "I've **decided** to wear my sneakers to the picnic."

deep Deep means from the top of something to the bottom, but the word is usually used about holes and things like that. If you step in a puddle and the water goes in your shoes, that means the puddle is **deeper** than your shoes are high.

deer A **deer** running free in the woods is a beautiful sight. **Deer** are tall, gentle animals. They eat grass and leaves and things like that. **Deer** are big, but they never pick on smaller animals.

delicious "This dandelion ice cream is **delicious**," says your friend. A food that is **delicious** tastes good to people, and makes them want to eat more of it. "May I have another helping of that **delicious** dandelion ice cream, please?"

delight What day was one of the happiest days of your life? Whatever day it was, it was a **delight** to you. A thing that is a **delight** is a thing that makes you happy and brings you a warm feeling of joy.

deliver "**Deliver** this porcupine to Polly Porter," says Peter Parker. **Deliver** has a lot of meanings, but the one most people use most often means, "Take this thing to the person who ordered it."

den A place where an animal goes to hide while he rests or sleeps is called a **den.** For a fox, a **den** may be a hole in the ground or a hollow tree. Maybe your father has a **den,** a small, quiet room where he can be alone.

dentist   A **dentist** is a doctor who is trained to take care of people's teeth. Pay attention to what your **dentist** tells you. If you don't have good teeth, you have to spend your life eating soup and oatmeal.

deny   "I **deny** it," says Harriet. "I did not hit Hank's hand." When you **deny** something, you say that it is not true. Always make sure that you are right when you **deny** something that somebody says.

desert   If you are the sort who gets thirsty a lot, stay away from **deserts.** A **desert** is a place where rain seldom falls, and the whole place is very dry and sandy. Some plants and animals have worked out ways to live quite comfortably in **deserts.**

desk People who work in offices usually work at **desks.** A **desk** is a kind of table with drawers to put things in. Some **desks** have computers on them.

dessert "I like the **dessert** part the best," you say. **Dessert** is the last part of the meal. It comes after the meat and the vegetables. **Dessert** is usually sweet. Cake or pie or pudding or ice cream is often served for **dessert.**

develop You and your friends are all **developing.** To **develop** means to grow and expand as much as is possible for you. Even after your body grows to its full size, your mind can continue to **develop.** It can continue to learn more and more.

different "My wagon is **different** from yours," says George. "My wagon has bigger wheels." A thing is **different** if it is not like other things of its kind. A green daisy growing in a field of white daisies would be **different.**

dig When you **dig,** you make a hole. If you want to make the hole bigger, you **dig** more dirt out. You can **dig** with your hands or with a shovel. **Digging** goes a lot faster when you use a shovel.

dime A **dime** is smaller than a penny, but a **dime** will buy ten times as much candy or anything else as a penny. The **dime** proves that size isn't everything.

dinner The biggest meal of the day is called **dinner**. Some people eat **dinner** at noon, and others eat **dinner** in the evening. Save your biggest appetite for **dinner**.

dinosaur Don't ask your mother if there were **dinosaurs** around when she was a girl. Your mother will not be pleased. **Dinosaurs** were large animals that lived a very long time ago. Brontosaurus was one of the biggest **dinosaurs**. A brontosaurus was about 70 feet long.

direction "You go down this street to the corner, and then you go left one block." The policeman is giving you **directions** on how to find your way. **Directions** tell you how to find something or how to do something. **Direction** means "go that way," or "this is how to do it."

dirty When you are **dirty,** you have **dirt** or grease or jam or some other kind of gick on you. A flower needs **dirty** feet but you will have to wash yours.

disappoint "I'm sorry I couldn't give you a horse for your birthday," says your friend. You were hoping he would give you a horse, but he didn't, and you are **disappointed.** If somebody thinks you are going to do something, but then you don't do it, you **disappoint** him.

discover If you find out how to grow square apples, you **discover** the way to do it. To **discover** is to find out about something. It is exciting to be a **discoverer.**

dish At dinner time, you put your dog's dinner in a **dish,** not in a bottle. A **dish** is deeper than a plate, and it has a big opening, so your dog can easily get his food. A thing you eat soup or cereal from is sometimes called a **dish** and sometimes a bowl.

dissolve When you put sugar in your lemonade and stir, the sugar seems to disappear. Actually, the sugar **dissolves.** When it **dissolves,** it melts and becomes part of the lemonade. Not everything will **dissolve.** Sand will not **dissolve** in your lemonade.

distance "How far is it to Ho-Ho-Kus?" asks your father. He wants to know the **distance.** When you know the **distance,** you know how far it is from one place to another place. The **distance** from where you are to the moon is about 250,000 miles.

99

dive Dive means to go headfirst into the water, instead of feetfirst. Don't **dive** into your bathtub. If you **dive** into a pool, make sure there is water in the pool, or you will be sorry.

divide If you have one pie and four friends, you try to **divide** the pie so everybody gets a piece, including you. It's hard to **divide** a pie into five pieces. It's easier to **divide** a pie into eight pieces. Invite three more friends.

dizzy When you turn round and round very fast, you get **dizzy.** When you are **dizzy,** things seem to be going around, and you have trouble standing up. Sometimes a fever can make you **dizzy.**

do Do is a little word that can mean a lot. Mostly, **do** means "get it **done**." Sometimes, to get it **done** can take a lot of **doing**. That would be true if you had to dry all the dishes after a big party.

doctor A **doctor** tries to help you get well when you are sick or hurt. A **doctor** can also tell you how to stay well. Listen to your **doctor**.

dog There is an old saying that a **dog** is man's best friend. **Dogs** and people have been friends for thousands of years. Wave to the next **dog** you see.

doll There are **dolls** that talk, or cry, or wet, or even walk, but they still are **dolls**. A **doll** is a toy that looks like a baby or a child or a grownup.

dollar "I paid four **dollars** for this fountain," says Frank. A **dollar** is a measure of money, just as an inch is a measure of how long something is. A **dollar** will buy the same amount of anything that 100 cents will buy.

donkey A **donkey** is an animal about the same size as a pony. **Donkeys** are big enough to ride on, but you can never be sure exactly where a **donkey** will go. They are very stubborn.

door A **door** is a thing that you are always on the wrong side of. If you are inside, you want to get out. If you are outside, you want to get in. A **door** will let you get in or out, unless the **door** is locked.

doorknob A **doorknob** is a round thing on a door that you have to use to open the door. If the **doorknob** is too high for you to reach, get your big brother to reach it for you. If you don't have a big brother, yell for mommy.

double If you are a twin, you know what **double** means. **Double** means two things that look so much alike it is hard to tell them apart. **Double** also means twice as much. A **double** ice cream cone is a cone with two scoops of ice cream instead of one scoop.

down You have to bend your head **down** to look at your feet. **Down** is the opposite way from up. **Down** is toward the ground or toward the bottom of something.

dozen "Give me a **dozen** cookies, please," you say to the storekeeper. **Dozen** means twelve. For some strange reason, nobody says, "It's a **dozen** o'clock," when the clock strikes twelve.

dragon **Dragons** are monsters that live only in storybooks. **Dragons** are huge. They have scales, and sometimes they have wings. There are **dragons** with lots of heads. A **dragon** can shoot fire out of its mouth or nose, but never out of its ears.

dream A **dream** is like a movie or a TV show that goes on inside your head while you sleep. Sometimes a **dream** is pleasant. Sometimes a **dream** is scary, and then it is called a nightmare.

dress A **dress** is a kind of clothing that girls and women wear. When a boy is told to get **dressed,** he puts on a shirt and pants. The bread and things that are stuffed inside a Thanksgiving turkey are called **dressing.**

drink "**Drink** your orange juice," says your uncle Fred. **Drink** means to swallow something wet like water or milk. **Drink** can also mean the stuff you swallow. "May I have a **drink** of root beer, please?"

drizzle When it is not raining hard, but just coming down in slow little drops, you say it is **drizzling.** A **drizzle** is a very light and gentle kind of rain. Wear your raincoat. It might rain harder.

drop If you hold a bowling ball in your hands and then let it go, the bowling ball **drops.** **Drop** means to let something fall down to the ground, or the floor, or as far as it can go. Don't ever **drop** a bowling ball on your feet.

drum A **drum** is a hollow thing that makes a noise when you hit it with a stick or something else. If someone gives you a real **drum,** don't cut the top off to see what is inside. There is nothing inside.

dry After you come out of the bathtub, you get **dry.** You wipe all the water off you with a towel. A thing that is **dry** has no water or moisture. Cake doesn't taste very good when it gets **dry.**

duck A **duck** is a largish bird that can swim very well just by moving its feet. A **duck's** toes are connected together with skin, and it can't walk very well on land. A **duck** can swim better than you can, but you can walk better than a **duck** can.

during "I'll eat my popcorn **during** the movie." **During** means while something else is going on. It is not polite to eat popcorn **during** the time your dentist is trying to fix your teeth.

dust Dust is a lot of very tiny bits of things that float around in the air and collect under the bed. When your mother tells you to **dust,** you clean the **dust** off furniture and floors.

duty If it is your job to feed the zebra every day, it is your **duty.** A **duty** is something that you are supposed to do, and everyone expects you to do it. It is your **duty** to always tell the truth.

dwarf A fully grown thing that is very small for its kind is called a **dwarf.** A child who is three feet tall would not be called a **dwarf,** but a fully grown tree that is only two feet tall would be called a **dwarf.**

abcd**e**fghijklmnopqrstuvwxyz

each "Give **each** man a sword," yells the captain. **Each** means every one of them. If there are red jelly beans, and yellow ones, and blue ones, and black ones, and you say, "Please give me one of **each**," you want one of every kind.

eagle **Eagles** are large birds with strong wings and very good eyes. **Eagles** can fly high and see very far. The bald **eagle** is a symbol of the United States. A bald **eagle** isn't really bald. The feathers on this **eagle's** head are white, and that is why it looks bald.

ear The part of your **ear** that does the most work is not the part that you can see. The part of your **ear** that sticks out from your head collects sounds and sends them inside your head where other parts of your **ear** really do the "hearing."

early If the turtle race is supposed to start at two o'clock, and you arrive with your turtle at one o'clock, you are **early.** If you get someplace before you are supposed to be there, you are **early.** It is better to be **early** than late.

earth The stuff that grass and plants and trees grow in is called **earth.** The planet we all live on is called **Earth.** We must take very good care of our **Earth.**

east If you stand facing the place where the sun rises every morning, you are facing **east.** **East** is a direction. If you start walking **east,** and walk long enough, you will come to the Atlantic Ocean. Take your swimsuit.

easy "Sure, I can do that. It's **easy**," you say. **Easy** means it is not hard at all for you. Maybe it's hard for your friend to run two miles, but it's **easy** for you because you have practiced.

eat Nobody has to be taught to **eat**. **Eating** comes naturally. When you **eat,** you put food in your mouth, chew it, and swallow it. There are proper manners of **eating,** however. People would think it strange if you lapped up mashed potatoes with your tongue.

egg An **egg** is a marvelous thing. Out of an **egg** comes a living creature. Chickens and all other birds lay **eggs**. So do fish, frogs, turtles, snakes, and alligators. Giant dinosaurs laid giant dinosaur **eggs**.

eight **Eight** is a word that tells you how many. **Eight** means seven and one more. The numeral that stands for **eight** is 8. If your friend tells you he has **eight** puppies, you know he has a lot of puppies.

either "You can have **either** this jackrabbit or this jackknife," says Uncle Jake. **Either** means one or the other. You can't have both.

elbow The place where your arm bends in the middle is called your **elbow.** When you bend your **elbow** there is a bone that sticks out. When you bump this bone in a certain way, it tingles and hurts. This bone is called a funny bone. It ought to be called an unfunny bone.

elephant If anybody offers you an **elephant**, don't take it. You would wear yourself out just carrying water to your **elephant**. An **elephant** drinks about 20 buckets of water a day. An adult **elephant** is the biggest living land animal.

elf An **elf** is a storybook creature that looks like a small human being. **Elves** have pointy ears and are supposed to have magic powers. They guard pots of gold, and things like that. In Irish stories, **elves** are called leprechauns.

elk An **elk** is a large kind of deer that lives in cold parts of the United States and Canada. These **elks** have very large antlers. There are people who belong to a club who call themselves **Elks.** They do not have antlers.

empty   When there is no more milk in your glass, the glass is **empty.** If somebody gives you a piggy bank, it is **empty.** You are supposed to **empty** your milk glass and fill your piggy bank.

encourage   The word **encourage** has the word **courage** in it. When you **encourage** somebody, you try to give him **courage** to keep going. "That's the way," you call. "I know you can do it."

end   When the movie is finished, the words on the screen say "The **End.**" When you walk out on a diving board until there is no more diving board, you have come to the **end.** It's odd, but a piece of string has two **ends,** and they both look alike.

enjoy You **enjoy** foods that taste good to you, or things that make you feel good. You can **enjoy** jumping into a big pile of autumn leaves. **Enjoy** is a happy word.

enough "No, thank you. Four helpings of burned marshmallows are **enough,**" you say. When you have **enough,** you don't want any more or need any more.

enter "Come in," says your friend. You open the door and **enter.** To **enter** means to go in. A place where you **enter** is an **entrance.**

entertain A magician pulling flags out of his ear **entertains** you. He makes you laugh, or makes you want to see more. A thing like a circus or an ice show is an **entertainment** because you want to see everything that is going on. A thing that is **entertaining** is not boring.

entire If your cat swallows a whole fish, it swallows the **entire** fish. An **entire** class is the whole class, with nobody missing. **Entire** means the same thing as complete.

equal You have three field mice, and your friend has three field mice. The two of you have **equal** numbers of field mice. Things that are **equal** are the same in some way or other. If you can run just as fast as your friend, you are **equal** in running.

equator If the Earth wore a belt, the belt would go around the **equator**. The **equator** is an imaginary ring around the Earth halfway between the North Pole and the South Pole. It's very cold at the North Pole and the South Pole, but it's very hot along the **equator**.

equipment When you decide to climb that steep mountain, you will need lots of **equipment. Equipment** is all the stuff you need to do something. When you and your family go camping you need **equipment** like a tent, a stove, food, and other things.

error If you mean to put ketchup on your hamburger but put it in your milk instead, that is an **error.** An **error** is a mistake that you didn't mean to make. You are in for a surprise when you drink your milk.

escape If your kangaroo jumps over the fence and hops away, he **escapes.** **Escape** means to get away from people who are trying to keep you penned up. The next time you are captured by bank robbers, try to **escape,** and call the police.

evaporate Put some water in a saucer, and leave the saucer on a table. In a day or two the water is gone. It **evaporated.** When water **evaporates,** it slowly turns into tiny, invisible drops, and the drops float off in the air. Almost any liquid will **evaporate.**

evening "Please come to my party tomorrow **evening,**" says Gloria. In most places, **evening** means that time of the day when the sun is going down. But in some places, **evening** means any time between the middle of the day and the night. Maybe you had better ask Gloria what she means.

event Anything that happens is an **event,** especially if it is the kind of thing you remember. If it snowed six feet on your birthday, that would be an **event.** People would talk about it for years.

ever "If you **ever** find a green rabbit, let me know," your friend writes. **Ever** means always or at any time. "If you **ever** need help, let me know," Grace says.

examine When you take a watch apart to find out what makes it tick, you **examine** it. **Examine** means to look at a thing very closely to find out all about it. A doctor **examines** you when you are sick to try to find out why you are sick.

excellent "This swordfish stew is **excellent**," you say. You think it is the best swordfish stew you ever tasted. A thing that is **excellent** is better than others of its kind.

excuse "Please **excuse** me for sitting on your hat," you say. You are asking the person to forgive you for your mistake. "I didn't know the hat was there." That is an **excuse.** That is the reason why you are asking the person to forgive you.

exercise Running, jumping, swimming, climbing, skating, and swinging are all ways of **exercising.** When you **exercise,** you use your muscles, and you make your body work harder. Everybody needs **exercise.**

exhausted After you do too much exercising, you are **exhausted. Exhausted** means too pooped to do anything more. Your legs feel like heavy logs, and your eyelids keep trying to close. When you are **exhausted,** go to bed.

exit The door where you go into the haunted house says "Entrance." The door where you go out says **"Exit." Exit** means either the place where you go out or to go out. If you are in a hurry to get out of a place, look for an **exit.**

expect "I **expect** that my camel will be here shortly," Jean says. She thinks that any minute now her camel will come over that sand dune. Something you **expect** to happen is something you are pretty sure will happen.

experience "That sled ride was a great **experience,"** Danny says. He was there, and he did it. He felt the cold, he smelled the fresh air, and he heard the snow crunch under his sled. Anything you do and hear and feel and see and smell is an **experience.**

explain When you tell your friend exactly how you built your igloo, you **explain** how you did it. You tell it so clearly that he learns how to build his own igloo. Now **explain** why you built your igloo.

explore If you row a boat over to that island and walk everywhere on it to find out what is there, you **explore** the island. An **explorer** is somebody who wants to find out about things. Every kid is an **explorer** at heart.

extra "Here's an **extra** bun," the baker says. You went to the store for a dozen buns, and then the baker gave you one more. That one is an **extra** bun. It is more than you asked for. When you try harder than people expect you to, you give **extra** effort.

extreme If the weather gets so hot that you can fry hamburgers on the sidewalk, the heat is **extreme.** The word **extreme** means very, very much so.

eye Your **eyes** are the most marvelous cameras in the world. Your **eyes** take hundreds of pictures in a minute, and send them into your brain for you to see.

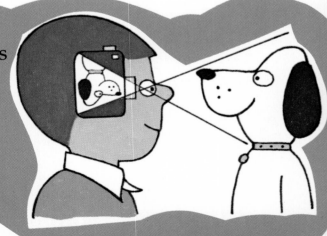

abcde**f**ghijklmnopqrstuvwxyz

face A mirror shows you your **face.**
Your **face** is the front part of
your head, and is the place where
your eyes, nose, and mouth are.
A clock is peculiar. It has
hands on its **face.**

fairy A small, imaginary,
human-looking thing with
wings is called a **fairy.**
A **fairy** is supposed to be
able to do all sorts of magic
things. A tooth **fairy** is
supposed to put money under
your pillow after one of
your teeth comes out.

fall When you bump a glass off
the table, it **falls.** A **falling**
thing **falls** down until it can't
fall anymore. Your glass stops
falling when it hits the floor.
You stop **falling** when you hit
the floor, too.

false A thing that is not true is **false.** If you stick a mustache on your upper lip, that mustache is **false,** because you did not grow it yourself. If you tell your friend a giraffe ate your hat, that story is **false,** unless a giraffe really did eat your hat.

family Your mother and father and brothers and sisters are your **family.** They are called your immediate **family,** or your closest **family.** Your grandparents, aunts, uncles, and cousins are also part of your **family.**

famous If everywhere you go people say, "That's Fanny Franklin," you are **famous.** A person who is **famous** is well known to lots of people for having done something important.

127

far "I can't get to your house in ten minutes, because Africa is too **far** from here," Chris says. Something that is **far** is a long way from where you are.

farm If you want to see how peas, pigs, and potatoes are grown, go to a **farm.** A **farm** is a place where plants and animals are raised for food or for clothing. A **farm** is a place with lots of space, and lots of work.

fast If you can beat every other kid in putting on your boots and jacket, you are **fast.** Don't be too **fast** when you cross the street. Take time to look both ways.

fat A bear that has eaten so much honey he can't get into his cave is **fat**. A thing that is **fat** is bigger around than it ought to be. Extra food gets turned into **fat**. **Fat** is the soft white stuff you see on meat.

father A male parent is a **father**. If you are a boy, you might become a **father** when you grow up. Then people will give you presents on **Father's** Day.

favor "Will you do me a **favor** and hold my fish?" Fred asks. A **favor** is a kind thing you do for somebody, or that somebody does for you. If you hold Fred's fish while he finds his frog, you are doing Fred a **favor**. Always be willing to do a **favor** for a friend.

feathers Any animal with **feathers** on it has to be a bird. Birds are the only creatures who know the secret of growing **feathers**. **Feathers** are light, and they are warm. An elephant would look silly with **feathers**.

feel "This rock **feels** rough," Kate says. She **felt** it with her hand. When you **feel** something, you touch it. Maybe the thing **feels** cold or smooth or wet or hairy.

feet The things you stand on are your **feet**. Sometimes you put your **feet** in socks and shoes, and sometimes you don't. Think of what trouble a centipede would have if he put shoes on all his **feet**. Think of how many shoelaces he would have to tie.

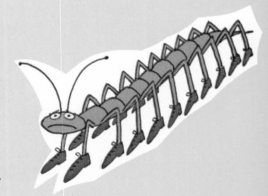

female   Your mother is a **female.** If you are a girl, you are a **female.** When you are fully grown, you will be a woman.

fever   You should stay in bed when you have a **fever.** When you have a **fever,** your body feels hotter than it usually does. You are sick. Stay in bed if you have a **fever.**

few   When you have eaten all but three of your jelly beans, you have only a **few** jelly beans left. **Few** means not very many. If you had a thousand jelly beans, you would have a lot of jelly beans, not a **few.**

field A large, flat piece of land with no trees on it is called a **field**. A **field** is a good place for growing corn or cows, or for playing some games. It would be dangerous to play football on a **field** filled with trees.

fight It is never pleasant to see a **fight.** Sometimes people get angry with each other, and they yell at one another or hit one another. That is **fighting.** There is usually a way to keep a **fight** from happening. Look for that way.

find When you lose the key to your bubble gum bank, you look for the key until you **find** it. Sometimes you **find** something you were not even looking for. "Look at the horseshoe I **found,**" you say.

fingers Those things sticking out from your hands are **fingers.** If you are like most people, you have five **fingers** on each hand. One **finger** is different from the others, and is called a thumb.

fire Cooking hot dogs over a **fire** is a fun thing. A **fire** is hot, and a **fire** gives off light. A **fire** can be useful, and a **fire** can be dangerous. Don't play with **fire.**

first If you are standing in line to see the horror movie and everybody else in line is behind you, you are **first.** When you are the **first** one to cross the finish line in a race, you win **first** prize.

THE SCARY GHOST

fish Your **fish** lives in a different world. Your **fish** lives in a world of water. A **fish** can breathe in water, but it cannot breathe in air. Try to imagine how different your life would be if you were a **fish.**

five If you have four buzzards and then get one more, you will have **five** buzzards. **Five** is the number of toes you have on each foot, unless you have weird feet. The numeral that stands for **five** is 5.

fix "I can **fix** that clock," you say. You know how to make the clock all right, so it will work again. Take the mouse out of the clock, and probably that will **fix** the clock. It will go again.

flat A table is **flat,** and a pancake is **flat,** and most walls and floors are **flat.** A thing that is **flat** is not rounded like a ball, and does not have ups and downs. It is straight and even.

flavor When your friend says, "I like the taste of this ice cream," she means she likes its **flavor. Flavor** is the way a thing tastes. Peppermint and chocolate are two very different **flavors.**

float Your raft **floats** on water because it is lighter than water. A rock does not **float** because it is too heavy. A rock sinks. A gas-filled balloon will **float** in the air if you let it go. A thing that is **floating** just sort of drifts around.

floor   If you are inside your house, the thing you are standing on is a **floor.** If you go downstairs and look up at that **floor,** it is now a ceiling. You are standing on a different **floor. Floor** is down, and ceiling is up.

flower   A **flower** never grows on a frog or a cow, only on a plant. Not every kind of plant grows **flowers,** but most do. From **flowers** come seeds which can grow to be new plants.

fly   A **fly** is a little insect that bugs you in the summertime, and **fly** is what a giant jet airplane does. **Fly** is a little word with a lot of meanings. On breezy days you can **fly** a kite.

follow Your friend whispers, "**Follow** me. I know where the treasure is hidden." You **follow** her. You go where she leads you. To **follow** is to go behind someone who is leading the way.

food What you eat at meals is **food.** Vegetables, meat, bread, milk, and pudding are all **foods.** Sticks and grass are **foods** for some kinds of creatures, but not for you. Don't eat them.

for "This present is **for** you," says Uncle Frank. That means it is meant to be yours. You go to the store **for** popsicles. **For** is a little word with a lot of meanings. You can think **for** hours about all the ways you can use **for.**

forest Lots and lots of trees growing close together are a **forest**. It is usually cool and shady and quiet in a **forest**. A **forest** is a great place to go exploring in, but be careful not to get lost. After a while, all the trees in a **forest** look alike.

forget If you **forget** what **forget** means, you **forgot**. **Forget** means you don't remember something you once knew. "Who invented the toothpick?" asks your teacher. "I **forget**," you say. Try to remember.

fork Don't ever try to eat soup with a **fork**. **Forks** leak badly. A **fork** has sharp points called tines or prongs. A **fork** is great for spearing meat or potatoes. Use a spoon for soup or ice cream. Spoons don't leak.

four If you are **four** years old, you are one year older than when you were three. **Four** is three and one more. **Four** is the number of legs on your cat or your moose. The numeral that stands for **four** is 4.

fox A **fox** is a wild creature that looks like a smallish dog. **Foxes** and dogs are related. A **fox** is thought to be very clever at tricking his enemies. A person who is good at outsmarting other people is called **foxy.**

free "These balloons are **free**," says the balloon man. "You can have any that you want without having to pay for them." A bird that is not in a cage is **free.** Any creature that is **free** to decide for itself has **freedom.**

freeze Can you hold water in a sieve? Yes, if you **freeze** the water. When you **freeze** water, you make it so cold that it turns into ice. Then it is **frozen.** Any liquid will **freeze** if you can get it cold enough.

friend "Pluto is my **friend,**" you say to Ann. **Friends** are people who like each other and who like to spend time together. **Friends** help each other in times of trouble. The best way to make **friends** is to be **friendly.**

frog To look at a **frog,** it is hard to realize that he started as a thing that looked like a fish. Then the **frog** had a long tail, but no legs. He lived in water, and was called a tadpole. Slowly, his tail disappeared, and he grew legs. He climbed out on land and was a **frog.**

from "I just came **from** Germany," says Jack. **From** means "the place where I was before I started my trip." **From** can also mean because of. "I'm tired **from** chasing all those pirates."

frost The beautiful white stuff that you find on your window on a cold winter morning is **frost. Frost** is a lot of tiny drops of water that stick to the window and freeze. If you live in a place where it never gets cold enough, you never get to see **frost.**

fruit Apples, peaches, bananas, and strawberries are all **fruits.** Usually when people talk about **fruit,** they mean sweet, juicy things that grow on trees or other plants. Almost nobody calls a tomato a **fruit.** But a scientist does. To a scientist anything with seeds in it that grows on a plant is a **fruit.** Even a nut is a **fruit.**

full If you can't pour any more juice in your glass because it would run over, then your glass is **full**. A thing that is **full** can't hold any more. If you eat ten hamburgers and three ice cream cones, you probably feel **full**.

fun Anything you do just because you like to do it is **fun**. A circus or a boat trip you enjoy is **fun**. Anything that makes you laugh is **funny**.

fur The hair that grows on a bear, a rabbit, a raccoon, or any other animal is called **fur**. If the hair that grows on your head also grew all over you, you would be called **furry**. If you had **fur,** you wouldn't have to buy a winter coat.

abcdef**g**hijklmnopqrstuvwxyz

game "I just invented a new **game**," says Abner Doubleday. "It's called baseball." A **game** is a fun thing people enjoy playing. Also, a **game** has to have rules that everyone agrees on. Checkers is a **game** almost anyone can play, and the rules are easy to learn.

garden If you plant flowers or radishes or cabbages, you make a **garden.** If other plants start to grow in your **garden,** they are weeds. Pull the weeds out of your **garden** so your **garden** plants have a better chance to grow.

gather "I am **gathering** eggs for my egg coloring party," Horace says. When you **gather** things, you bring them together. A family **gathering** is a time when the family **gathers** together.

genius If someone says, "You are a **genius**," that is a compliment. A **genius** is someone who is extra smart. If you invent a car that runs on spinach instead of gasoline, people will call you a **genius**.

genuine "That pearl is **genuine**," Paul says. **Genuine** means real and not fake. A race horse is a **genuine** horse, but a merry-go-round horse is not a **genuine** horse.

gerbil Don't expect to see much of your **gerbil** during the day. Most **gerbils** prefer to sleep during the day, and to run around at night. **Gerbils** are members of the mouse family. Feed your **gerbil** seeds.

get "I'll **get** the ice cream cones," you say. **Get** means you will take them from the ice cream man. When you **get** something, that means now you have it. Now, do you **get** the meaning of **get**?

ghost Nobody has ever proved that **ghosts** are real. A **ghost** is believed to be the spirit of a dead person. It is said that **ghosts** can do scary things like floating through walls and rattling chains. The next time you see a **ghost,** tell him, "BOO."

giant A mouse big enough for you to ride on would be a **giant** mouse. A **giant** thing is anything that is extra big. If you grow to be as tall as a tree, people will call you a **giant.**

gift "This puppy is my **gift** to you," Harvey says. Another word for **gift** is present. When you give somebody a **gift,** the **gift** belongs to him, and he can do what he wants to with it. People give you **gifts** on your birthday.

giraffe Be sure to build a very tall house for your **giraffe.** A **giraffe** is the tallest animal there is. The long neck and the long legs of a **giraffe** are what make it so tall.

girl It is not true that **girls** are made of sugar and spice and everything nice. **Girls** are made of the same stuff boys are made of. The big difference is that a **girl** grows up to be a woman, and a boy grows up to be a man.

give When you **give** a blue rabbit to your friend, that means the blue rabbit is now his. When you **give** something, you don't control it any more. When you **give** the blue rabbit to your friend, you show that you believe your friend will take good care of the blue rabbit.

glad "I'm **glad** you came to my party, Gladys," you say. You are happy she came. **Glad** and happy are two words that mean almost the same thing. "I'll be **glad** to help you paint the house," you say to your father. You are happy to help.

glass **Glass** is stuff that breaks quite easily. Windows are made of **glass,** and so are most bottles and drinking **glasses.** Be careful with broken **glass.** It is sharp.

glue Do not put **glue** on your father's chair, because when your father stands up the chair will stick to him. **Glue** is stuff that makes things stick together. **Glue** is very useful when you use it properly.

go "I will **go** to the moon next week," you say. **Go** means to move, usually from one place to another. If you say, "My mule won't **go**," that means he won't move at all. Get a better mule.

goat Some people say a **goat** will eat a tin can. This is not true, but a **goat** will eat just about anything else. In many parts of the world, **goats** are raised for their milk or their wool. **Goats** look quite a bit like sheep, so don't get confused when you go to buy a **goat**.

goldfish Your **goldfish** is not rich just because he has the word **gold** in his name. A **goldfish** gets its name from its orangish color, which looks like **gold.** Other than that, a **goldfish** is just a plain old fish.

good "This ice cream is **good**," you say. It tastes the way you want it to taste. A thing that is **good** is the way you want it to be. We don't all think the same things are **good.** Do you think snails taste **good?**

goose If a large bird walks up to you and says "Honk" in a loud voice, that bird is a **goose.** Maybe "Honk" means "Hello" in **goose** language. There are wild **geese** and tame **geese.** Tame **geese** are raised on farms for food.

gorilla Gorillas are just too big. A **gorilla** is a member of the monkey family, but he is the biggest. A **gorilla** is too big to keep around the house.

grand There are lots of words that really mean big, and **grand** is one of them. But **grand** can also mean something else. **Grand** can mean super. You probably had a **grand** time at the circus.

grandfather Your **grandfather** is your father's father or your mother's father. If you are a boy, you might be a **grandfather** someday. If you have a child and that child grows up and has a child, you will be a **grandfather.**

grass If you have a yard, the green stuff that grows on it is **grass.** Be kind to your **grass.** The **grass** family is perhaps the most important plant family in the world. Wheat and rice and corn are all **grasses.**

gravity When you let go of a stone, the thing that pulls the stone down to the ground is **gravity. Gravity** is a force that you can't see or hear or smell, but it is always there. When you trip over a rock, you fall down. **Gravity** pulls you down. You never fall up.

great Something that is **great** is something you will remember for a long time. "That was a **great** camping trip," you say. A **great** thing is big or important. You may grow up to be a **great** man or woman.

green "My cat is **green**," Henry says. Henry has a strange cat. **Green** is a color usually found on plants. Grass, tree leaves, and most other plants are **green.** If you want to make **green,** mix together blue and yellow paint.

ground When you step off the sidewalk, you are on the **ground.** Another name for **ground** is earth or dirt. **Ground** is what grass and trees and other plants grow in. Your house is built on the **ground** unless you live on a houseboat.

group "This is a nice **group** of kids at my party," Cindy says. A **group** is a bunch of people or of things that are alike in some way. You could call a bunch of grapes a **group** of grapes if you wanted to.

grow **Grow** is what you are doing. A thing that is **growing** is getting bigger. When you can't get your old shoes on because the shoes are too tight, it is not because your shoes became smaller. Your feet **grew** bigger.

guess If you don't know how many beans are in the jar, you have to **guess. Guess** is what you have to do when you don't really know. Sometimes you **guess** right and sometimes you don't. "**Guess** what I found," says George.

guest "Your **guest** is very polite," your father says. A **guest** is someone who is visiting at your home. If you have a **guest,** you are a host. You are supposed to make your **guest** feel welcome.

guide "I'll **guide** you to the pirate cave," you say. **Guide** means to show the way. You know where the pirate cave is, but your friend doesn't. You **guide** him there.

guilty If you are the one who ate the cake for the party, then you are **guilty.** A **guilty** person is a person who has done something he shouldn't have done. If you are **guilty,** the best thing to do is to admit it.

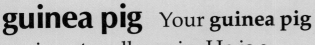

guinea pig Your **guinea pig** is not really a pig. He is a member of the mouse family. Introduce your **guinea pig** to a real pig, so he can see what a real pig looks like.

guitar A **guitar** is an instrument for making music. Most **guitars** look a bit like overgrown violins. Play your **guitar** with your fingers. Play your violin with a bow.

gull If your **gull** refuses to eat hamburger or birdseed, it is because he would rather eat fish. **Gulls** live around oceans, and they are good at catching fish and other seafood. A **gull** is a largish bird with a big beak and a loud voice.

gum You can chew chewing **gum** for an hour and it still stays **gummy.** If you chew bubble **gum,** you can blow bubbles. **Gum** can also mean the part of your mouth that holds your teeth.

abcdefg**hi**jklmnopqrstuvwxyz

habit If you always put your right shoe on before you put your left shoe on, that is a **habit**. A **habit** is something you do all the time and without thinking about it. If you always put a carrot behind your ear, people will say that is a weird **habit**.

hair The stuff on top of your head is **hair**. **Hair** is friendly. **Hair** keeps your head warm in winter, and it keeps the sun off in summer. Take good care of your **hair**. Wash your **hair** and brush it. If you ever lose your **hair,** you will be bald.

hamburger "My favorite food is **hamburger**," Jeff says. There is no ham in a **hamburger**. All the meat is beef. The **hamburger** gets its name from the German city of Hamburg, where it is said the first **hamburgers** were made.

hamster A **hamster** is a smallish pet that lives in a cage. **Hamsters** are not good for much except being **hamsters.** They are very good at that. **Hamsters** are members of the mouse family, and they are gentle creatures.

hand "Give me a **hand,**" Herman says. Herman has two **hands,** but he needs another one to help him hold his tiger. Your **hands** are two of the most marvelous things ever created. Your **hands** can do things no other animal's **hands** or paws can do.

happen "I saw it **happen,**" says Harriet. To **happen** simply means to **happen.** There is no other good word to use for it. If you are outside, and it **happens** to rain, you get wet. A thing that **happens** is sometimes called a **happening.**

159

happy You know when you are **happy**. You smile or laugh, and you feel good. A friend coming to see you can make you **happy**. When you do something nice for your parents, you make them **happy**.

hard "This sidewalk is **hard**," Horace says. When he fell down and hit it, the sidewalk didn't bend like a soft pillow does. A thing that is **hard** doesn't bend when you push on it. Walls and floors and rocks are **hard**.

hat A thing that is meant to be worn on a head is a **hat**. **Hats** come in many different shapes. Some **hats** keep off the sun, some keep off the rain, and some keep you warm. Some **hats** are just meant to look pretty. A person who makes **hats** is a **hatter**.

have When you **have** something, that thing is yours. If you **have** a camel, you **have** to figure out what to do with your camel. **Have** sometimes works with other words. ''I **have** been to the zoo three times,'' you say. The next time you go, leave your camel there.

he A boy is a **he,** and a man is a **he. He** is a word that stands for a male creature. ''I gave my purple penguin to **him,**'' you say. **Him** is a word that is used instead of **he** at certain times. Now the purple penguin is **his.** You probably already know when to use **he, him,** and **his.**

head Your **head** is that roundish part on top of your body where your face is. Your brain is in your **head,** and that is why people say, ''He has a good **head** on his shoulders.'' If you are the leader of a club, you are the **head** of the club.

hear **Hear** is what your ears do. They take in sounds and pass them on to your brain. Rabbits and donkeys must have very good **hearing.** Look at the size of their ears.

heart You have a marvelous pump inside of you that works all the time. This pump is called your **heart.** Your **heart** pumps blood all through you. Your **heart** is about as big as your fist.

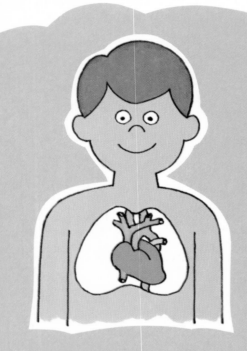

heavy "This is a **heavy** hammer," Jack says. He can hardly lift it. A thing that is **heavy** weighs a lot. Large machines can lift very **heavy** loads. As you grow older, you will get taller and **heavier.**

help When a swimmer in the water yells, **"Help!"** that means he is in trouble. He needs somebody to come and save him. "Please **help** me rake the leaves," your friend says. She wants you to do part of the work.

hen Any bird that lays eggs is a **hen.** Usually, though, people mean a female chicken when they say **hen.** Be thankful for the **hen.** If **hens** weren't so good at laying eggs, you couldn't have fried eggs for breakfast.

here "Please bring the wagon **here**," you say. **Here** is the place where you are. Every other place is there. When you leave **here,** you go there.

163

hide "I will **hide** behind this bush," Betsy says. When you **hide** something, you put it someplace where other people won't see it or find it. It is not a good idea to **hide** your snowballs in the oven. They will melt.

high A kite way up in the sky is **high.** So is an airplane or a cloud. **High** means up there pretty far. When the grass gets **high,** you have to mow it. A tree is **higher** than a bush.

hill A **hill** is a bump on the earth that never got big enough to be called a mountain. You could say a **hill** is a smallish mountain. **Hills** are good for sled riding, if you live where there is snow.

hippopotamus Never try to put a **hippopotamus** in your bathtub. **Hippopotamuses** like water, but most of them are much too big for a bathtub. The rest of your family would probably be angry if they went to take a bath and found a **hippopotamus** in the tub.

hit Swing a bat and **hit** a ball. **Hit** means to knock something real hard. When you fall down, you **hit** the ground. That **hit** hurts you, but it doesn't hurt the ground.

hold It is hard to **hold** water in your hands, because the water sneaks through your fingers. When you **hold** something, you grab it and hang on to it. Your dog likes to **hold** onto a stick.

hole The way to make a **hole** is to take all the dirt out of it. The more dirt you take out of a **hole,** the bigger the **hole** gets. It is hard to figure out a way to carry a **hole** from one place to another.

home **Home** is where your family is, and where people are always glad to see you. Your **home** might be a house or an apartment in a big building. Wherever your **home** is, it is the place where you belong.

honest A person who is **honest** tells the truth and does not take things that do not belong to him. A person who tells lies or who steals things is not **honest.** That person is **dishonest.** It is much better to be **honest** than **dishonest.**

hope "I **hope** it will be sunny for the turtle race tomorrow," Joe says. A **hope** is a kind of wish. When you really want something to happen, you **hope** it will happen.

horse Don't ask for a **horse** for your birthday unless you have a lot of space and a lot of grass. It is not a good idea to try to keep a **horse** in your bedroom. **Horses** are big animals, and they make a lot of noise. **Horses** wear iron shoes.

hot Some days in summer, when the sun is shining, you feel **hot**. You are sweaty, and you want a cool drink. A pot of food cooking on the stove is **hot**. A thing that is **hot** is more than just warm. It is **hot**.

hot dog   A **hot dog** is not a dog that is hot. A **hot dog** is a long, skinny meat thing that usually is inside a bun. **Hot dogs** are served at picnics, parties, and ball parks. Do not put too much mustard on your **hot dog** or you will be sorry.

house   "My **house** is red," Rose says. A **house** is a building that protects people or things from the sun, rain, or snow. In a zoo, lions live in a lion **house.** Maybe your dog lives in a dog **house.**

how   "**How** high can you jump?" Bob asks. When **how** starts a sentence, it asks a question. When **how** comes in the middle of a sentence, it means this is the way to do it. "I'll show you **how** to catch an octopus," you say.

168

huge A thing that is **huge** is even bigger than big. Three scoops of ice cream on an ice cream cone would be big, but thirteen scoops would be a **huge** ice cream cone. Don't try to eat an ice cream cone that **huge.** You might get a **huge** bellyache.

human You are a very special kind of creature called a **human.** Only **humans** can talk about all kinds of things, think about all kinds of things, and make all kinds of things. There are small **humans,** big **humans,** and **humans** of different colors, but they are all **humans.**

hungry After a long day of swimming, running, or playing ball, you are **hungry.** When you are **hungry,** any kind of food smells good. You just want to eat. After you eat a lot of food, you aren't **hungry** any more.

hunt If you lose your golden egg in the grass, you have to **hunt** for it. When you are **hunting** for something, you are trying to find it. You **hunt** for it until you find it.

hurry "I am in a **hurry**," you say. "I have to catch that bus." A person who is in a **hurry** doesn't have time to stop and talk. He has to move fast. He will miss that bus if he doesn't **hurry.**

hurt Bang your toe on a rock, and your toe **hurts.** You know when you **hurt.** "Ouch!" is what people yell when they **hurt.** Happily, most **hurts** don't last very long. After a while, your toe won't **hurt** any more.

abcdefghijklmnopqrstuvwxyz

I There is no word that is any shorter than **I. I** is small in size but big in meaning. **I** means the person who is talking. **Me, my,** and **mine** are other words that stand for **I.** "That is **my** flying saucer."

ice There are times when you want **ice.** You want **ice** when you have a new pair of **ice** skates and you want to try them out. You want **ice** to cool your lemonade on a hot summer day. You do not want to see **ice** in the water when you want to go swimming.

ice cream Some words fool you. **Ice cream** is not made of ice. **Ice cream** is made of milk or cream, sugar, and flavoring. All this is mixed together and then frozen. It has to be stirred all the time while it is freezing. Making **ice cream** can be hard work.

idea Cartoonists often draw a light bulb over a person's head to show the person just had an **idea**. An **idea** can be a sudden thought that pops into your mind. An **idea** might be something you have thought about for a long time. "I have an **idea** about how to make a windmill car," you say.

if When something isn't exactly true yet, but it might be or could be true, you use the word **if**. "**If** I had a helicopter, I could fly over that mountain," you say. You don't have a helicopter. But **if** it came true that you had one, you could fly over the mountain.

igloo People who live in **igloos** seldom buy air conditioners. An **igloo** is a house built of blocks of snow or ice. Eskimos used to build **igloos,** but now most Eskimos prefer to live in wooden houses.

173

ill When you are **ill,** you have a fever, or you hurt, or something else is wrong. Another word for **ill** is sick. A person who is **ill** has an **illness.** Get rid of it, and you will feel better.

imitate If Amy barks and creeps on her hands and knees, people will say she is trying to **imitate** her dog. **Imitate** means to try to act like something or somebody. Try to think of a way to **imitate** a flower opening up.

immediately "Come out of that tree **immediately!**" says the ranger. **Immediately** means right now, not ten minutes from now, but right now. If you don't get out of that tree **immediately,** you could get hurt. Somebody is cutting that tree down.

immense Our language has lots of words that mean big, but **immense** means extra big. **Immense** means so big you wouldn't believe it. "His hat was **immense**," you say. His hat was five feet tall.

important "It's **important** that I get there in time for the bus," you say. It matters a lot. If you miss the bus, you can't go on the zoo trip. A thing that is **important** has to be done. A person who is **important** matters a lot to other people. You are **important** to your parents, and they are **important** to you.

impossible "That's **impossible**," people used to say. "Nobody can get to the moon." A thing that is **impossible** can't be done or can't happen. But astronauts did get to the moon. If you think something is **impossible**, keep on trying. Maybe you will find out it is not **impossible** after all.

in When you are not out, you are **in.** Some stores have two glass doors marked **IN** and **TUO.** You are supposed to go **in** the door marked **IN.** When you are **in** the store and look at the other door, it now says OUT. Another word for **in** is inside.

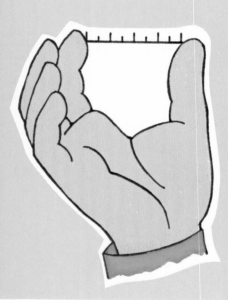

inch An **inch** is this long ——————. Nobody knows exactly why. Twelve **inches** makes a foot, which is probably longer than your foot. An **inch** is just a way of measuring how long or how tall something is. In Canada an **inch** is 2.5 centimeters.

include "Let's **include** Rob in our snork hunting party," you say. When you **include** someone or something, you bring it in as part of a group. If you get a new wheelbarrow, you can **include** it in your wheelbarrow collection.

incomplete If you build a chair but forget to put on the legs, the chair is **incomplete.** A thing is **incomplete** when it does not have all its necessary parts. An elephant without a trunk would be an **incomplete** elephant.

increase "My, how you've grown," says Uncle Oscar. When you grow, you **increase** in size. To **increase** means to add to or to make bigger. Some parents put marks on a wall to show how a kid is **increasing** in height.

innocent "I didn't eat that swordfish," you say. "I'm **innocent.**" **Innocent** means not guilty of having done something wrong. When you are **innocent,** you don't even know about the wrong thing. Ask the cat who ate the swordfish.

insect An **insect** is a smallish creature with six legs. Some people call them bugs. There are more kinds of **insects** than any other kinds of creature. **Insects** are all around you. People who study **insects** are called entomologists.

instead "I'd like to have apple pie **instead** of spinach pie," says Brenda. The menu has spinach pie, but she would rather have apple pie. When you say "I want this thing **instead** of that thing," that means you want this thing but not that thing.

intelligent If people say you are **intelligent,** they think you can learn things quickly. If you are very good at solving problems, you are **intelligent.** The world never has enough people who are **intelligent.**

interest If somebody gives you a book about snakes, maybe that book will give you an **interest** in snakes. When you are **interested** in something, you are curious about it and want to find out more about it.

into "I am going to put this lemon pie **into** this pillow case," George says. **Into** means inside of. It is not a good idea to put the lemon pie **into** the pillow case. Put the lemon pie **into** you. Eat it.

introduce When you **introduce** people, you say, "Jill, this is Jack. Jack, this is Jill." To **introduce** means to tell each of two strangers who the other one is. After you **introduce** them, they aren't strangers to each other any more. Tell Jack and Jill to be careful with that pail of water.

invent "Look at the four-wheeled baseball bat I **invented,**" Walter says. When you **invent** something, you make something nobody ever saw before. You are the first person to make such a thing. Maybe people will like Walter's **invention,** and maybe they won't.

invisible "How do you like my **invisible** car?" Fred asks. A thing that is **invisible** is a thing that can't be seen. But just because you can't see it doesn't mean it isn't there. Air is **invisible,** but it is all around you.

invite When you **invite** someone, you ask him to come to your party or to join your club. You send an **invitation,** "Please come to my pea picking party." The person you **invited** will come if he likes you or if he likes to pick peas.

iron Try picking up metal things with a magnet. If a thing sticks to the magnet, it is made of **iron,** or it has **iron** in it. **Iron** is a silverish metal. **Iron** is used in making cars, stoves, refrigerators, and many other things. You would not like an **iron** pillow.

is "What **is** it?" you ask. **Is is** one of those tiny words that **is** hard to explain, even though you use it all the time. "He **is** purple," you say. **Is is** the word that hooks the words "he" and "purple" together.

island A hunk of land with water all around it is called an **island.** If you fall off a ship, look for an **island.** An **island** is a better place to be than out in the water.

it When you don't know what to call a thing, you can always use **it**. "Where did you find **it**?" you ask. Or you say, "**It** is raining." What is raining? **It.** You are lucky to know the word **it,** because you can use **it** for almost anything.

itch You know when you **itch.** When you **itch,** you feel like you have to scratch. An **itch** is a tingly feeling on the outside of you somewhere. A mosquito bite **itches.** Don't scratch that mosquito bite too hard or you might make it **itch** worse.

ivy **Ivy** is a green plant that won't quit. **Ivy** keeps on growing. It grows straight up walls, or it grows along the ground. **Ivy** doesn't seem to care. If you could ever stand still long enough near an **ivy** plant, the **ivy** would probably grow up on you.

j J k K k
j J k K
K j J

abcdefghi**jk**lmnopqrstuvwxyz

jar   A **jar** is a round glass thing with a fairly big top and a lid. Pickles usually come in **jars.** Never put your hand in a **jar,** unless you are sure you can get your hand out. If you have to walk around with a **jar** on your hand, people will stare.

jaw   Put your hand under your chin and pretend to chew. The part of your face that moves is your **jaw.** Your **jaw** is the only bony part of your face that can move. Be thankful for your **jaw.** If you didn't have your **jaw,** you couldn't chew food.

jelly   "I like **jelly** on my mashed potatoes," Linda says. Linda is unusual. **Jelly** is a clear, sweet, squishy stuff made of sugar and some kind of fruit juice. Most people put **jelly** on bread and toast. Jam is a lot like **jelly,** except that jam is made with whole fruit instead of just fruit juice.

GRAPE JELLY

job "I can't talk to you now. I have a **job** to do," you say. You have to wash that pig until he is clean. A **job** is something you have to do. Do a good **job** of washing that pig.

join "We would like you to **join** our taffy pulling club," says Patsy. When you **join,** you become a member of a group. To **join** means to bring things together. Sometimes people **join** together to clean up a dirty neighborhood.

joke A **joke** is a story or a trick that is supposed to be funny. But people don't always agree on what is funny. Maybe your father doesn't think it is very funny if you fool him with a stick of pepper-flavored chewing gum.

jolly If you laugh a lot and are happy most of the time, people will say you are **jolly.** Turtles seldom seem to be **jolly.** Nobody can figure out why. People who are **jolly** have more friends than turtles do.

journey "I am going on a **journey** to Kalamazoo," you say. When you go on a **journey,** you go from one place to another place. A **journey** is a trip, usually a long trip. You often need maps. A trip to the grocery store is a kind of **journey,** but not much of one.

juice If you squeeze a fruit or vegetable real hard, **juice** comes out. It's pretty easy to squeeze **juice** out of an orange, but it's pretty hard to squeeze **juice** out of an onion. Most people would rather drink orange **juice** than onion **juice** anyway.

jump Everybody knows how to **jump,** but it's hard to explain it. You push yourself up into the air with your feet and legs. Frogs and grasshoppers are the best **jumpers.** If you could get a frog to explain **jumping** to you, probably you could become a champion **jumper.**

jungle "I hope there are no tigers in this **jungle,**" Mary says. A **jungle** is a hot place with trees and bushes and vines all over the place. It rains a lot in a **jungle.**

junk "I don't want that **junk,**" you say. "I don't want a broken light bulb and a worn-out sneaker." **Junk** is stuff that is no good any more. Getting rid of **junk** is getting to be a big problem, because there is so much of it.

kangaroo A **kangaroo** is an animal with very long back legs, short front legs, and a pocket in the middle. **Kangaroos** can travel fast by making long jumps. If you had a **kangaroo** to ride, you could get places in a hurry.

keep "I'm going to **keep** this rabbit," Ralph says. He is not going to give it to anybody. When somebody asks you, "Can you **keep** a secret?" that means can you **keep** the news to yourself and not give it to anybody else. Sometimes it is hard to **keep** a secret. You have to **keep** your mouth shut.

ketchup That thick red stuff you pour on a hamburger or a hot dog is called **ketchup.** Some kinds are called **catsup,** which is even sillier. **Ketchup** tastes great on some foods, but it's terrible on chocolate cake.

kick A one-legged man can't **kick** a ball. To **kick,** you have to be able to stand on one foot and hit the ball with the other foot. A mule **kicks** with two feet. Anybody who has ever been **kicked** by a mule remembers it for a long time.

kid It used to be that **kid** meant a young goat. Today **kid** also means a child. Even children call themselves **kids.** If you are a **kid,** just remember there is some difference between you and a young goat.

kind A person who is always polite and helpful to other people is called **kind.** There is another word **kind,** which means that sort of thing. "I like that **kind** of cake," you say. Always be the **kind** of person who is **kind** to other people.

kitchen A **kitchen** is where all the cooking goes on. When you are hungry, the **kitchen** is the best place to be. There are lots of ways you can be helpful in the **kitchen**.

kite "My **kite** is up so high I can hardly see it," Sam says. Wind is what holds a **kite** up in the air. **Kites** come in many different sizes and shapes. There are even **kites** big enough to lift a person up in the air. That can be a dangerous way to fly.

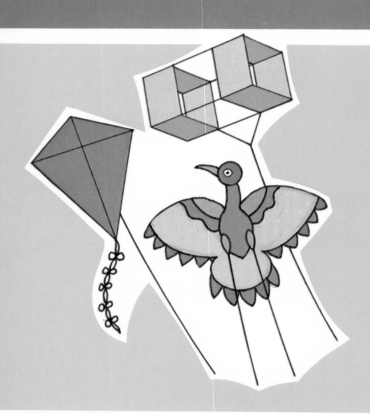

kitten Give up trying to teach your **kitten** to bark, because your **kitten** is a young cat. No cat has ever learned to bark. **Kittens** are playful and friendly.

knee   The place where your leg bends in the middle is called your **knee. Knees** are great, because they make walking much easier. If you try walking without bending your **knees,** people will say you walk like a robot.

know   "I **know** what chocolate tastes like," you say. You **know** because you have tasted it before. You **know** what your house looks like. You **know** the sound of your friend's voice, you **know** the soft feel of cotton, and you **know** the smell of popcorn. If you have learned to swim, you **know** how to swim.

koala   To keep a **koala** happy, you need a eucalyptus tree. **Koalas** like to eat the leaves of eucalyptus trees. But eucalyptus trees grow in Australia. A **koala** looks like a cute teddy bear. Or you might say a teddy bear looks like a cute **koala.**